WonderWorks

Decodable Reader

Unit 7

Mc Graw Hill

Contents

Rick Did It!
by Anita Monroe
illustrated by Linda Bleck
1

Fun in the Sun
by Helen Lee
illustrated by Anni Matsick
9

Kip Can Wag!
by Leonard Butler
illustrated by Jan Pyk
17

Rick Did It!

by Anita Monroe
illustrated by Linda Bleck

Pack the black sack Rick.
Flip the flap.

Pack a bat and a hat.
Do not pack a cat.

Slip in a snack.
Pet the **little** cat.

See the red clock!
Flip a flap and go.

Get a cab **with** Mom.

Rick hit it!

He ran and ran.

Rick did it!

Fun in the Sun

by Helen Lee

illustrated by Anni Matsick

Bud can run up to Pat.
Pat can pet Bud.

Lad can run up to Pat.
Pat can pet Lad.

Bud can nap and nap.
Lad can lap it up.

Bud and Lad can run **for** fun.
Bud and Lad can dip in.

Mom and Dad **have** fun.
Pat and Bud **have** fun.

It is fun in the sun!

Kip Can Wag!

by Leonard Butler
illustrated by Jan Pyk

Meg and Gus can see Kip.
Kip is on top **of** the big rug.

Did Kip run?

They can not see Kip!

Kip is not on the big rug.
Gus can pat it.

Kip got in the rug!
Kip hid in it!

The rug can wag!
It is Kip in the rug.

Meg can hug Kip.
Gus can pet Kip.
Kip can wag!

Unit 7

Word Count: 51

Decodable Words

Target Phonics Elements: Blends *bl, cl, fl, sl*
black, clock, flap, flip, slip
Review: *bat, cab, cat, get, hat, hit, in, it, Mom, pet, red, Rick, sack*

High-Frequency Words

he, little, with
Review: *a, do, go, see, the*

Word Count: 67

Decodable Words

Target Phonics Element: Short *u*
Bud, fun, run, sun, up
Review: *can, Dad, dip, in, it, Lad, lap, Mom, nap, Pat, pet*

High-Frequency Words

for, have
Review: *and, is, the, to*

Word Count: 66

Decodable Words

Target Phonics Elements: Initial and Final /g/*g*, Consonant /w/*w*

big, got, Gus, hug, Meg, rug, wag

Review: *can, did, hid, in, it, Kip, not, on, pat, pet, run, top*

High-Frequency Words

of, they

Review: *and, is, see, the*

Decoding skills taught to date:

Consonants /m/*m*, /s/*s*, /p/*p*, /t/*t*; Short *a*; Short *i*; Initial and Final /n/*n*; Initial /k/*c*; Short *o*; Initial and Final /d/*d*; Consonant /h/*h*; Short *e*; Blends *sn, sp, st*; Consonants /f/*f*, /r/*r*; Initial and Final /b/*b*; Consonant /l/*l*; Initial /k/*k*; Digraph *ck*; Short *u*; Initial and Final /g/*g*; Consonant /w/*w*